POP, R&B, AND GOSPEL DRUMMING

CHRIS JOHNSON

Co-written by Nik Preston

Foreword by Rickey Minor

I0808635

To access audio and video visit:
www.halleonard.com/mylibrary

Enter Code
2769-1338-6949-5583

ISBN 978-1-5400-4583-6

HAL•LEONARD®

Visit Hal Leonard Online at
www.halleonard.com

Contact us:
Hal Leonard
7777 West Bluemound Road
Milwaukee, WI 53213
Email: info@halleonard.com

In Europe, contact:
Hal Leonard Europe Limited
42 Wigmore Street
Marylebone, London, W1U 2RN
Email: info@halleonardeurope.com

In Australia, contact:
Hal Leonard Australia Pty. Ltd.
4 Lentara Court
Cheltenham, Victoria, 3192 Australia
Email: info@halleonard.com.au

CONTENTS

DEDICATION

This book is dedicated to my late father, Pastor Albert "Al" Johnson Jr., for his example of discipline, work ethic, and musical background. Without your example, I wouldn't be able to share what I have and who I am. Thank you, Pop.

ACKNOWLEDGMENTS

Recorded at Clear Lake Recording Studios, North Hollywood

Audio Engineer: Eric Milos

Assistant Audio Engineer: Paul Sukontapirom

Mixing and Mastering: Kyle Hamilton

Videography: Kenneth F. Washington, Xavier Pierre Conley

Photography: Cameron Dantley

Cover Photography: Alex Solca

Drum Transcriptions: Alex Silvergold

Drum Technician: Eric Parker

Chris Johnson is represented worldwide by NPA Management Ltd.

www.npamanagement.co.uk

Berkeley Suite, 35 Berkeley Square

Mayfair, London, UK, W1J 5BF

Tel: +44207 692 8242

Chris Johnson endorses Yamaha drums, Sabian cymbals, Remo drumheads, and Vater drumsticks.

remo.com

FOREWORD

Long before Chris Johnson could write *this* good book, he was a young man raised with and rooted in *the* Good Book.

I first met Chris Johnson as he was coming onto the pop scene, looking for gigs in the secular world. I was looking for a young drummer to work with Mya, a new artist who was about to do a series of television performances to promote her new album. I asked my drummer Teddy Campbell if he had any recommendations, and he said, "I know this young drummer from church—he can play in *any* world he chooses."

He was right—Chris is one of those drummers who just feels right *instantly*. Some musicians come in and have to warm up to a new situation. He has the ability to come in pretty hot. *Whatever* he plays feels good right away, and I think that's because for Chris, it's always about the music first. Honestly, for a lot of players, especially drummers, it's about impressing the other musicians in the band. Chris comes in and lays *down* the groove. He understands that everyone will be remembered for their contribution to the overall sound. It's not about being the *baddest*—it's more about playing what the music and the artist needs.

Chris was really quiet at first. I soon realized that it was *not* about him having a shy personality, but because he took the time to soak in everything around him. He was slow to speak and quick to *listen*. Because he had not grown up around R&B and pop music, Chris really had to listen, learn, and appreciate the new musical worlds he was becoming a part of. So when he went out into the musical universe of being a professional musician, he had the talent and the temperament to blossom in any situation. I found myself using him whenever the opportunity was available.

Chris quickly became one of the most in-demand drummers, working with the likes of Stevie Wonder, Jennifer Lopez, Rihanna, Lady Gaga, and many more incredible artists. Chris could handle all of that because, like all the greatest drummers, he has his own innate sense of time and groove that he takes wherever he goes.

Coming from the church, there were times when he seemed surprised that not everybody was always trying to be uplifting. He would call me for advice, and I believe these life lessons have found their way into not just the music, but also into his growth as a human being. Chris has maintained his kindness as he has expanded his musical talent and continued his ongoing success story. That's because he now understands a big secret—that getting the *call* is a great accomplishment, but an even greater one is getting the call *back*.

This book is a must-read for all aspiring musicians. His approach to music and life is transforming.

Today, Chris is a great musician who is able to go anywhere he wants to, yet still grounded in his core beliefs as a musician and man. Chris Johnson will be a true leader wherever his exciting musical life takes him.

Rickey Minor

INTRODUCTION

Welcome to *Pop, R&B, and Gospel Drumming*! I've been blessed to have a career that has taken me all over the world, playing music in stadiums and arenas, on albums, films, and awards ceremonies, and working with wonderful artists along the way, some of whom have been my musical heroes. In this book, I go into great detail about my experiences playing with pop artists and superstars along with my background as a church musician growing up in Los Angeles. I've also included some transcriptions of my playing on music by pop and R&B artists I've worked with over the last 20+ years in addition to some of the original music with my group Legally Blynd.

ABOUT THE AUDIO AND VIDEO

You can access the audio and video content by going to *www.halleonard.com/mylibrary* and inputting the unique code printed on the first page of this book.

Each transcription comes with accompanying audio tracks and videos to aid you in your own practice and learning. This book also includes several video interviews with myself, top session musicians featured in the video performances, and key industry figures from various parts of today's scene. These professionals include:

Aaron Spears

Brian Frasier-Moore

Bryan "B-Dub" White

Eric "Pikfunk" Smith

Nate Watts

Errol Cooney

Kamil Rustam

Lonny Bereal

Rickey Minor

Kevin Teasley

I hope that this book provides insight for your own playing and development and that each person who reads this is left inspired to chase after their own dream, in their own way.

PART 1: TECHNIQUE, STYLE, AND THE MUSIC INDUSTRY

TECHNICAL DEVELOPMENT

The topic of technical development is unique for me, as I'm a self-taught drummer from Los Angeles. What you would consider technical, I consider *groove*. I learn and play everything mostly by ear, which has led me to hearing a song once and be able to play it comfortably the next time around. That's how I was taught to play, and it requires a certain element of playing from the heart. Now, after being required to learn a large amount of music over the past 20 years, I've gained a better understanding of the technical side of playing in different styles. Each gig is different; they call for any number of things. For example, pop sounds are different than those of R&B, and gospel has continued to evolve over the years. It's just that simple: identify the genre, pick your sounds, and then move to the next phase.

Placement is highly important when it comes to mastering technique, as your placement varies when you play certain styles of songs. I'm naturally left-handed, but I grew up playing a right-handed kit. In my early years of playing drums, I wasn't taught how to use traditional rudiments, so I played what I heard with whichever hand felt comfortable and learned from there. There were no rules because I taught myself. Later, certain gigs called for electronic parts, and I had to re-learn how to play again. Most of the gigs from 2006–2015 emphasized a heavy use of electronics. I had to bring my hands to even strength while keeping the live element present in the groove. I've been adding these elements more and more to my playing, making me the player I am today. There is no single right way to play drums; it's more important to achieve a comfortable balance with your hands and feet while you play. Here are some exercises that will help you strengthen your hands and be more balanced in your playing.

HAND STRENGTHENING EXERCISE

KICK/SNARE EXERCISE

The number of strokes on the drum you play can be very technical. Playing a combination of single and double strokes in different places of the groove is very technical. Controlling every note with finesse and dynamics are all needed to develop your technique. The foundation of everything is great timing, knowing where all the beats are at all times. You should be able to feel the kick drum as your own heartbeat, no matter what tempo, whether it's "dog, I'm tired" slow, or "too fast for no reason" fast. Being in tune with the pulse can help you do anything. On some gigs, you don't have the luxury of leaning on the hi-hats to keep time. Certain parts of the show are so magical that they don't need the hi-hat present at all. Our timing must be absolutely LOCKED, with a metronome and without. (It's actually better to be able to play without a click; instead of relying on the click, we must be locked with our inner clock.)

A key in developing my technique was being able to play fills within a technical groove, with hits and specials that enhance the song. In your own playing, it's important to break these grooves down to the basics. Then, playing fills within the groove becomes easier.

Here's an excerpt from "Umbrella" by Rihanna where I utilize fills within the hip-hop groove:

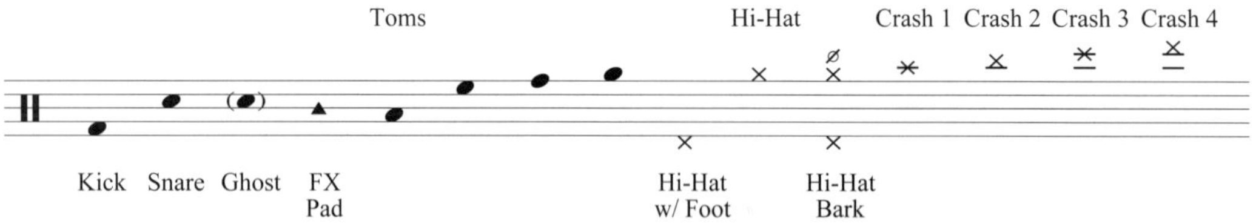

And here's a point where I use fills in a gospel context, within the song "Bump":

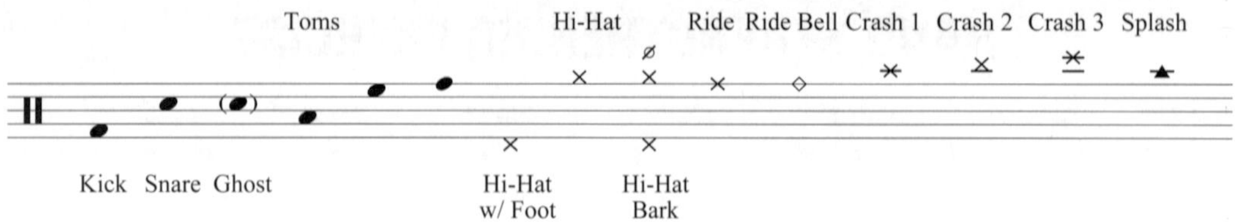

For more details and full transcriptions of "Umbrella" and "Bump," see Part 2 and Part 3, respectively.

There's an important difference in learning how to take the note away versus adding a note. For example, I prefer ghost notes to finesse a shuffle groove, such as a James Brown groove. But when you bring triggers and electronics into the mix of everything, single strokes will be your best friend. After a while, the use of single strokes, double strokes, buzz rolls, and ghost note combinations will allow you to develop your own technique, style, and identity in drumming.

One of my greatest learning tools was actually playing. In other words, on-the-job training was the best teacher. Nowadays, musicians have to deal with room sizes, acoustics, microphones vs. no microphones, small clubs vs. big clubs, theaters, arenas, stadiums, etc. All of these technical aspects will come into play. Learn to be sensitive to the room and how it relates to the dynamics of the song.

Placing your strokes in the center of the drums will help with technical development. Picture this: You're sitting in a club, and the drums are set up in a general way, but obviously, to the preference of the house drummer. There are usually stick marks on the drumhead that are about 3–5 inches in diameter. Oftentimes, the bigger the drum, the smaller the diameter. Hitting the center of the drum is the money spot and will help you get the most out of your drum. So try this: Set up a kick drum, snare, rack tom, and floor tom and begin playing double strokes, starting with the snare, rack tom, and floor tom. Start at a slow tempo, and then move faster when you're ready. Then, use single stroke-double stroke combinations. Each time you play your kit after playing these exercises, you'll see the improvements in hitting the center of the drum.

GROOVE DEVELOPMENT

Growing up in Los Angeles was tough. There were frequent drive-by shootings in addition to the presence of drug and alcohol addiction, gangs, and crooked cops and politicians. In the music industry, it was hard on me because there were tons of players, mainly drummers, that were killing the scene. I felt as though I couldn't play like those guys. They could move around the kit like Muhammad Ali; there was a certain beauty to the way they played. I would go to church and try all the fancy playing that my peers were doing, but I found that I struggled to meet their level, which affected my confidence for several years. I often questioned myself, asking, "Why can't I play like that?"

Coming from church, if there was a big concert or event happening, then all the musicians would gather around the band pit to get an up-close view of what was happening. In those times, I would sit on the drums before playing anything, already feeling defeated. My hands would cramp, and I would feel myself playing harder than I would usually play. I wouldn't be in control of my hands, notes, or anything else, resulting in me losing myself and my own identity while playing. At times, some people weren't so nice, and I'd hear, "He's not ready," "He can't play any chops," and "He's not good enough." Those times were grooming me for the real world.

I sat back one day, and it came to me—I could only be myself. When I'd struggled with my playing for a while, I used to only play the bare minimum so that the drums wouldn't get in the way of the groove or song. I started out with just the kick, snare, and hi-hat. I played the most basic beats at first, and then I began to develop my own voice by adding embellishments to the original groove, piece by piece.

Usually, the structure of a song is made up of an intro, verse, chorus, verse, chorus, bridge, and then an out chorus. Look at a song like a flight of stairs. To start with, you don't want to start running on the first flight. (Although you may be capable of doing so, it's not ideal.) Why? Because you may burn out too fast. On the first flight, establish the groove. When you come to the second flight, add just a little more flavor; you can do this by opening the hi-hats on grid of the beat. On the third flight, use what you've already played and add more to the groove without detracting from the song and or singer. Finally, on the fourth flight, add more energy through dynamics and embellishments.

Now, this is just the groove we're talking about. In the modern world of music, the demand for quality is staggeringly high. It's more than just groove; it's about the hits, stops, and accents. We must provide tasteful fills in and out of each section. So there needs to be a gradual build within the groove, something that says, "I'm here, but I'm not trying to be seen." Drummers have the hardest time taking notes away in order to play a groove or "pocket." The pocket refers to how the groove feels within the song. The pocket can be complicated or simple, but the foundation of building the groove is vital. Think of grooving like driving a car. Before you get to 60 mph, you have to pass 10 mph, 20 mph, 30 mph, etc. You can't skip any steps when it comes to building a groove. Make sure that every note means something and feels as if you have produced the song yourself. Care more about the overall picture than showcasing your own individual part. Overshadowing an artist can be selfish. If you are not the artist, then it's clear that it's not about you; it's about the front man or woman until it's your time, directing your own project and making your own decisions.

Start with a kick, snare, and hi-hat setup. This minimum set-up is what I call the "Tripod." By doing that, you've eliminated any extra or distracting elements. Just because we have a full setup of drums doesn't mean you have to hit all of them! If you can't play a song with only these three elements, then it means that you are too dependent on other drums to enhance the groove. There is no need to lean on anything other than the established groove played on the Tripod. Start by picking a groove at any tempo, simple or complex, and make sure that it is solid and steady. You'll find that the more comfortable you are with the Tripod, then the easier it is to move to the next phase. This is where you can add toms and other parts of the kit. When you play the toms, make sure they're rhythmically appropriate to the song; it's not wise to play a 32nd-note fill on a quarter-note groove.

Be careful—when you add a lot of notes, there's a chance that the groove can become too clogged. Without losing sight of the task at hand, add a cymbal or two and stick to the groove as best as you can. When the groove is established, survey the room. It's most likely that heads will be nodding, and there will be some foot tapping. As drummers and musicians, we have the responsibility to do our part and stay in our lane. The work you do won't go unnoticed by the other members of the band and the people in the audience.

My greatest groove building lesson was from Stevie Wonder. He used to come into rehearsal and teach the band a new song that he just wrote on the way over. Of course, he would start with me, being the drummer. First, he would tap on his legs and chest to show me the groove that he wanted. After I learned that part, I would continue to play until everyone in the band got their parts. Before I knew it, two or three hours had gone by, the entire time during which I had to play the same groove—no distractions, nothing extra, nothing more than what was needed.

By the time each band member got their parts combined into a well-arranged, brand-new song, I realized that as drummers, we must always be content with our part (the groove) and think about the bigger picture. It was an amazing experience to see a song broken down to that level. There was no click track; I had to turn up my sense of time and keep everyone together. So with grooving, you have to make sure that your timing is on point. Don't waver in the groove because the band is depending on you to stay the course and be as solid as a rock.

Pop, R&B, and gospel drumming is all relative as you may already know. These groove exercises will help you in all facets of playing. You still need all these tools for whatever is thrown your way. Try maintaining a level of calm so that you don't get ahead of or behind the beat. It's also important to learn how to adapt to what's happening around you. Approach each song like it's the last time you'll play and perform with the same conviction that inspired you to take up the drums in the first place. Be confident when you practice and be content if you're not featured in the spotlight.

GROOVE BUILDER 1

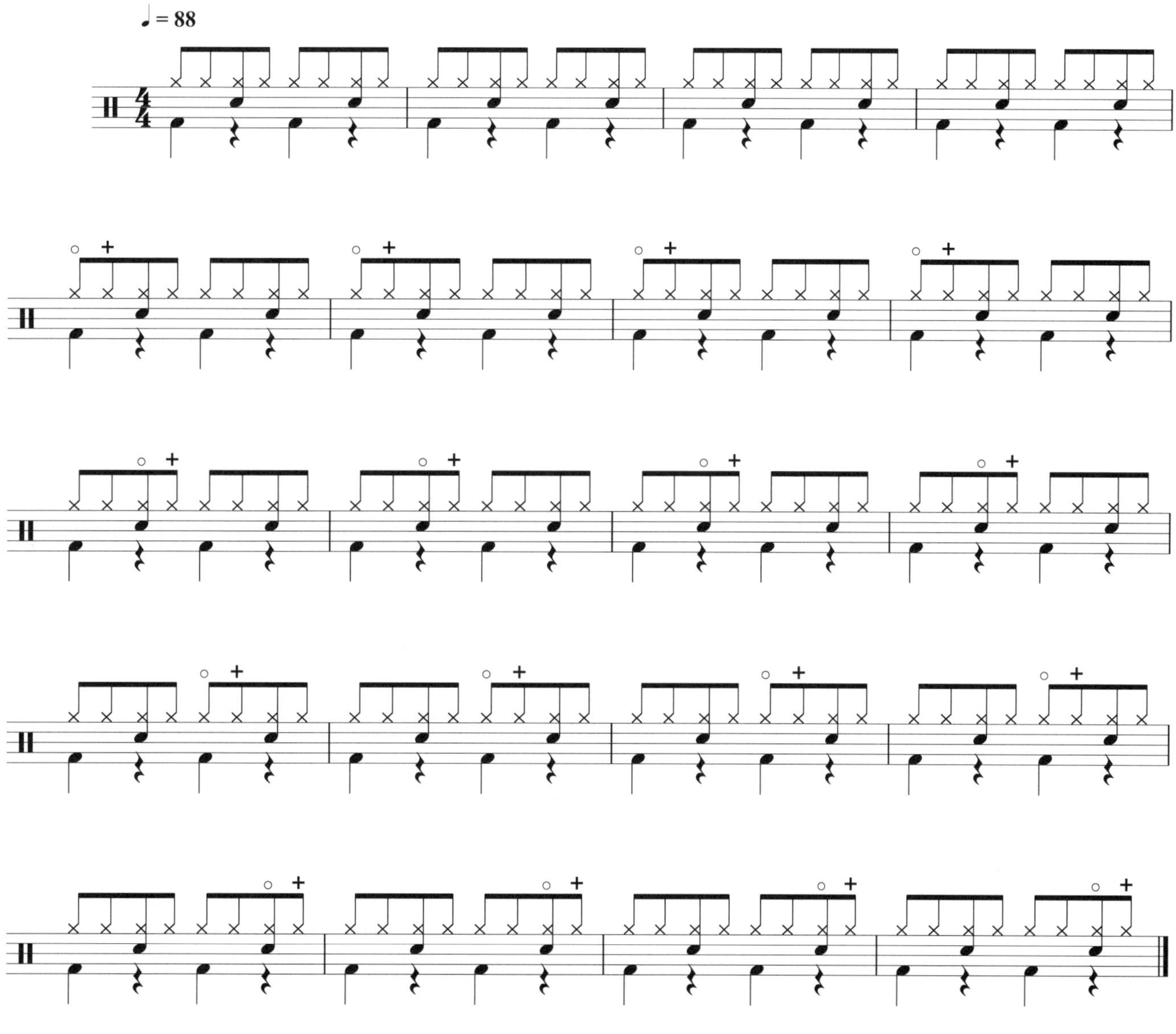

GROOVE BUILDER 2

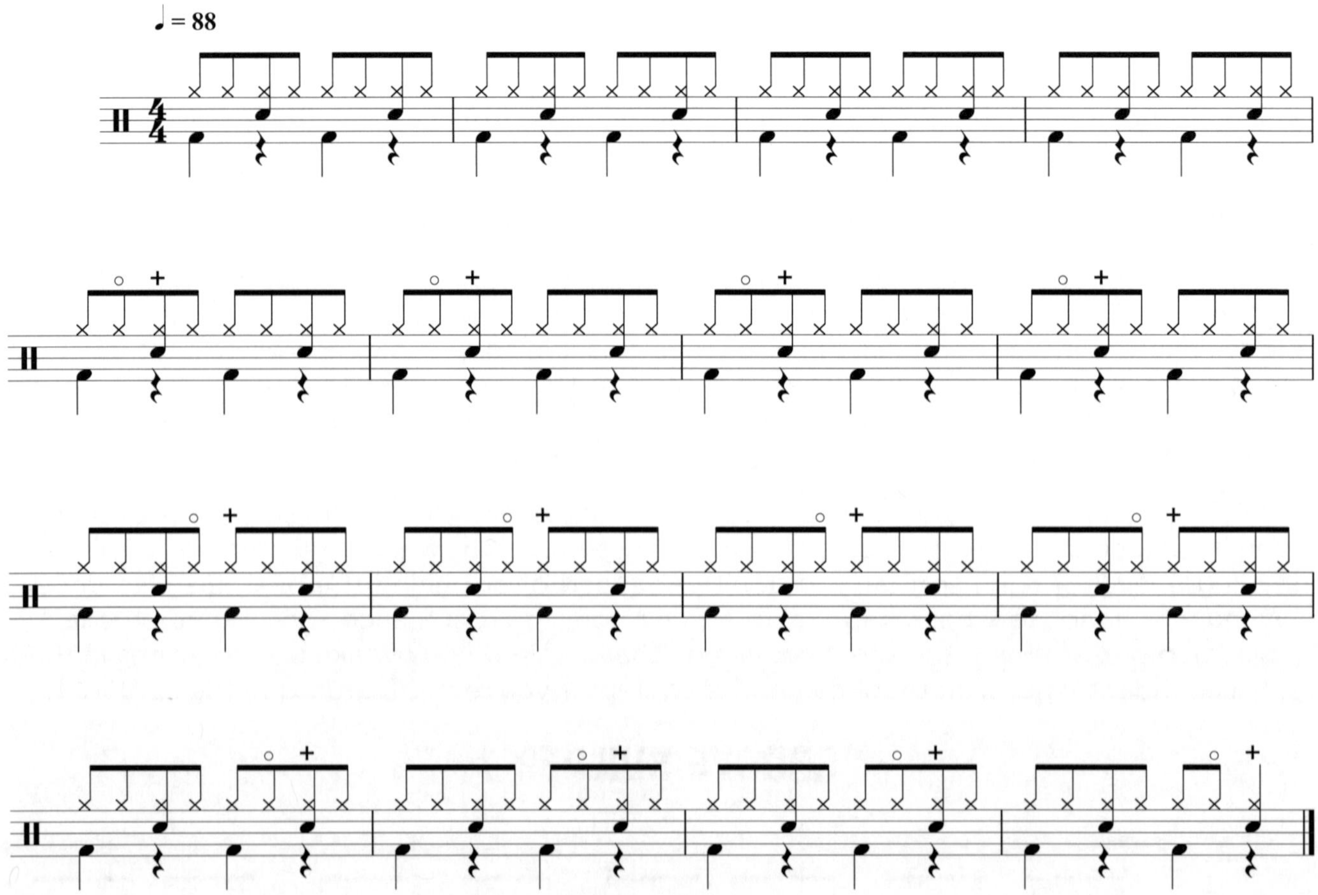

GROOVE BUILDER 3

GROOVE BUILDER 4

GROOVE BUILDER 5

STYLISTIC/GENRE AWARENESS

The more music you expose yourself to, then the more musical and stylistic awareness you gain in addition to expanding your musical vocabulary. This was especially true growing up in church, when my grandmother would randomly start a song, and we would be expected to join in without any preparation save for the many times we sang each song in past services.

Growing up, I played in church with just my uncle on guitar. I remember watching the feet of whoever was singing; at most times, they would pat their feet to the beat. It was hard at first trying to recognize 4/4 time signatures in addition to the most popular in the church, 6/4 time. Watching people clap their hands and stomp their feet helped me with my awareness within the music.

From birth to 18 years old, I could only listen to gospel music because of my dad and how he and my mother raised our household. It wasn't ideal for learning a bunch of music—I was stuck in one genre. However, gospel music at that time was diverse. John P. See, the Hawkins family, and Andre Crouch, to name a few, were the closest artists for me to be exposed to something outside of the traditional way of making church music. Funk and classical music were also played in our house. The sounds of the instruments were different, and they brought something unique to the table. My mom was a little more easy-going with the music, but only if my dad didn't find out. I got my first car and then started listening to the radio every day. Now, I understand this was only one style or genre of music, but it was the starting point of my learning and adapting to different things.

A little further into my years of playing, music became more structured and much less of a random song being sung. We had time to rehearse everything and work out any kinks within the arrangements. The tonal qualities of the instruments also help with genre awareness—piano, Fender Rhodes, Hammond B3 organ, guitar (dry), guitar with reverb, string bass, strings, horns, etc. Listening and paying attention to other elements will help you determine how to approach each song. The key factor is slowing your mind down to pay attention to all the elements, melodies, and voices. The more music you listen to, the more easily you will be aware of different musical styles. Eventually, it will become second nature.

It is also good to reference a song you may have heard before or a different mainstream artist/genre. I walked into a jam session one of the first times playing outside the church. The guy next to me was playing bass, and I asked him, "What song is this?" He replied, "You'll catch on—just think 'Motown.'" The only Motown songs I could reference were either by Stevie Wonder or the Temptations, which I heard on the radio!

I wasn't the best at knowing a wide variety of music, so as soon as I moved out of the house, I had tons of homework to do. I had to cram so much music in my brain like a test in grade school. It was hard attempting to listen to a bunch of music at one time. Gigs would come up, and I would stay up all night to make sure I was on-point for what was to come in rehearsal. I still lacked confidence, and I was unsure of how my approach would be accepted. My only solution was to rely on how I learned music in church. If I'm ever unsure about something, then I will strip everything down to the bare minimum and feel the song out before insulting or disrespecting the song itself. I take music very seriously and will do what's necessary to make the song feel the most authentic it can be.

That was my story 20 years ago, but now, there are still more styles and genres of music to explore. I'm still a student of music and will be ready for whatever is thrown at me in these genres. The same will be required of you in your own musical journey. After becoming well-versed in one thing, try not to solely dwell on that; there's so much more out there than your one favorite style of playing.

After gaining these tools and knowledge, you can become versatile over time. Versatility is the best way to keep you in the loop with current music. One of my busiest seasons was a two-year span during which I played on tour with Rihanna, and then Frankie Beverly and Maze right after. I toured with Seal during that time as well, and then right after that was a tour with Stevie Wonder. Each gig required me to know how to play and fuse all kinds of styles—pop, R&B, rock, fusion, funk, and classical.

PLAYING LATIN-INFLUENCED POP AND R&B

During my time with J-Lo, I had to play Latin grooves. My experience with Latin styles was pretty limited when I first landed the gig. Generally, I knew what **clave** was (e.g. 3:2/2:3 rumba), but **cascara** was something that was new to me.

I went home that night to dive into the music. With my left hand (since it's my strong hand), I played the cascara rhythm on the hi-hat and clave (3:2) on the snare side stick, or sometimes a wood block. Some of the syncopated parts actually made me count, which is something that I rarely have to do!

Here's an example of the cascara rhythm I play in "Havana" by Camila Cabello (the full song is in Part 2 of the book):

I can still remember one track where the cascara groove remained the same on the hi-hat and the clave changed to 2:3. It is fair to say I had a hard time catching it at first, but as always, after listening and repeating it over and over, it soon became instinctive. Every day in rehearsal or soundcheck, I would ask the musical director (MD) if we could play the Latin section of the show. That, coupled with a lot of practice sessions with the gifted and generous-spirited percussionist, Fausto Cuevas, got me up to speed (eventually!). Fausto spent so much time introducing me to **rumba** and **samba**, which is something I am ever thankful for and is still paying dividends.

For bass drum technique, I usually use my heel to play singles, but if there is a combination that needs to be played, then I use the slide (heel-toe) method to get some quicker action. I also use matched grip exclusively; it's the only way I know how to play, but I strongly recommend experimenting until you find something that feels natural. When playing ghost notes, I use a looser grip with more finger action.

Some people learn technique and apply it to the music, while others let the music shape their technique. For most of us, there's probably a middle ground, and I always see great players who have arrived at this from different schools of thought.

With the J-Lo show, I play a more "pop" style setup: 8", 10", and 12" rack toms and a 16" floor tom. I use a mid-tone snare (which for me is 14" x 5"), and just above the snare, I place the wood block. My cymbal selection is more or less suitable for a neutral sound. My cymbals include a 22" ride and crashes ranging from 20" to 22" and 19". The hi-hat size is 16", as I find it to be a nice universal sound for "Pop, R&B, and Gospel" drums.

TUNE MEMORIZATION

Growing up and playing in church, we didn't have sheet music because we didn't know how to read music. In fact, we didn't even have time to rehearse the songs half the time! I had to remember tunes by listening to lyrics. I didn't count bars, and I had no idea what key the song was in. For the most part, I didn't have a clue as to what was coming next. Each musician had what you would call "big ears." We would hear the song one time, and then we could be playing the very next time it came around.

My dad was a pastor at the time, so I didn't get exposed to any other music until I moved out of the house at the tender age of 19. At that point, I studied all kinds of music. Of course, that included the top 40 hits in the late '90s, but I also had to revisit songs and albums from the '60s and '70s. I had a bunch of homework to do.

During my first gig with charts, I panicked; I didn't know how to read or write music. I stared at the sheet music like a new born baby. Luckily for me, if we played the song a couple of times, then I would learn it by ear. It also helped hearing and recognizing the songs that I heard on the radio and the popular songs I saw on award shows and special musical events. Then, I'd go home and memorize the song and match the charts with the actual songs. Everyone in the band could tell that I couldn't read music, but I didn't embarrass myself too badly. Television shows like *The Four, Rising Star*, and *American Idol* only play songs off the top 40 list or classic songs like "Ain't To Proud To Beg" and "My Girl." It was a challenge at first; I didn't want to lose, so I had to study like never before.

I find the only way to truly memorize songs and grooves is to listen to what needs to be played. Memorizing one section at a time means that you can gradually put them all together, and before you know it, there's one song down! Developing your memory will help in the long run. With most of the big tours I've done, we will rehearse one to two months with just the band, and then we'll move to another month of production rehearsals. By then, I don't have to memorize too much because it's all muscle memory from that point. But don't be fooled by all the new changes—in most cases, things change last minute, even on stage. That's the time when to make sure all the little things are covered.

I have been blessed to have played so much music over the past 20 years. I've had to delete and reset my brain so many times. First, I'll play one show with an artist, and then two weeks later, I have to learn another show with another artist. Then, I go back to the beginning with the first artist, but this time, it's a new show. I know what you're thinking, "How could you play multiple gigs at the same time?" Indeed, it's a challenge, but it's doable! You have to really apply yourself to learning music and staying up-to-date in order to memorize something that you have to study. Music comes naturally to some people, but for others, not so much. Being able to adjust is key, but you only need that if you're not feeling comfortable. If you can prepare ahead of time, then please do. Even when you think you have it down, you still need to go over it one more time!

It's good to listen to the other elements in the songs and band; it helps with learning and memorizing tunes. Lyrics always come into play. When an artist is up singing, they don't want to have to think about bars and counts—they want to sing! The players in the band have so much more to worry about. For instance, in R&B, there's usually a break at the top of the second verse, so you are able to set up the break and move in and out of it. Or, a signature guitar riff can tell you when the next part is coming up.

It is also beneficial to break down the other instruments in the song when memorizing tunes. In the production phase of a recorded song, nothing is accidental. As a producer, you want to hear what you produced within a live version. It's important to not add unnecessary parts to a masterpiece; instead, you must respect what was composed and written. This means that all shakers and sound FX are in there for a reason and are therefore necessary. If it takes you a while to grasp the concept, then it's ok. Apply yourself and take the time to learn all sorts of songs and music. These tools will help with learning songs and breaking them down. Please don't get caught up in formulas, and don't assume that you know it when you actually don't. Do the work and expand your musical knowledge by learning as much music as you can. There's no single right way to learn music, but this has been working for me.

For some tours or gigs, we have to listen to the music on the way to the performance while traveling on a plane, train, or automobile. In one instance, I had just finished a tour in New York City, and I was on my way to the airport. I got a call from an old tour manager friend, who asked me, "Can you fly to Dubai tomorrow to do a show?"

I asked, "How long is the show?" (Of course, I asked how much it paid!) He replied, "It's an hour and a half show, and you will have to learn it on the way." After confirming that I had time to go home to Los Angeles and repack, I told him to send me the show, and I would take it from there. After sending my rider list over to him, we got started on listening to the music from New York to LA, all less than a day before getting on a flight to Dubai! I had to put everything in my brain aside to input all this music and data into my head to play a show. I also had to keep in mind that we would only have a soundcheck to get a small rehearsal in.

I didn't sleep at all for the 16-hour flight to Dubai. The show had about 20 songs, and I may have heard only three of them prior to getting the gig. I had to break down every song, starting with the kick and then the snare and hi-hats. I filled a notepad with as many notes as I could to guide me through all the material. We landed with a few hours to chill before the soundcheck. When I got to the room, I threw my bags down and turned the show's music back on to listen to before we left for soundcheck.

I didn't know anyone in the band; I spoke only to the MD through email. I was out there by myself, trying to bailout this artist and my friend the tour manager. I arrived at the stage for soundcheck and started setting up, still listening to the music. In case you didn't know, soundcheck almost never goes as planned. There are always technical difficulties, and you have to allow time for anything and everything to go wrong. Listening to the show's music and playing it are two totally different things. When tackling a new show, section, song, etc., you have to get your hands under it. All these grooves and songs are related, but they are also different at the same time.

Finally, I got back to my room, and I fell face-first onto the bed. (You can imagine how much of a toll this traveling and learning had taken on me over the last 32 hours.) On the next day, with rest and a clear head, I started focusing back on the show for the day. Once I heard the roars of the crowd, I knew I could rely on all those hours spent learning the songs to play them faithfully. When you've been playing drums for as long as I have, you get this "sixth sense" that everything will come out fine. In the case of this gig, I didn't play the show perfectly, but everyone was understanding. After all, I had to pull off an hour and a half show with less than 30 hours of preparation!

When playing drums or any other instrument, you have to be aware that things can change any moment. Sometimes, you will run into technical difficulties, equipment problems (most gigs won't have everything you play all the time), language differences, sleep deprivation, etc. Soundchecks can run long or late, and in-ear monitor levels may not be how they were in rehearsal. There are many variables to deal with, and musicians are at the front of it all. We have to hold our ground, and the key to memorizing tunes is all about preparation. All this preparation works as a preventative method to account for the last-minute changes.

I'm fortunate to have techs and assistants out on the road with me, but I still cannot rely only on them to make sure the show goes smoothly. If the call time is 12:00 pm, then I'm on my way by 9:00 am. I want to get to my gear in enough time to sit on the drums and make sure I'm comfortable, so I always take account for traffic or any travel delays. It's my goal to ensure that if any mishaps happen, it won't be from the drum department.

Finally, I can then grab a coffee or food and relax my mind. My mission is to not allow my day to drive me; I'm going to drive the day so I can be at my best when I approach my instrument. There are no excuses for me, and the same goes for YOU. Be at your best in preparation, and it will show on stage.

VOCABULARY ASSIMILATION

When starting or playing a groove, I always look at it like cooking. With some dishes, you're able to throw everything in at once and cook. With other dishes, you have to take time, adding here and there, tasting often. In your own playing, start from scratch and build the groove note by note, stroke by stroke. You can always add a little more, like blending swells and moments in the groove that could make a grown man cry. Essentially, it's like making a painting a little more lifelike. There is no need to rush to your favorite part of the song. It's an important, beautiful journey that's worth all the love and care.

It always helps to stop, listen, and then speak. Speaking only makes sense when there's no one else speaking. I believe vocals are the most important, and that is a good starting point. Let the artist and management ask for more if they want. They might say, "Everything sounds good, but can we get just a little more [insert request] from you?" This is how it usually goes. Then, you can go to your vocabulary bag and grab a little more to add to the song.

I practice practical, subtle things as well e.g. dynamics. Like I said earlier, dynamics come in many forms, and oftentimes, they occur in those live moments and real time. There are a lot of things you will not be able to prepare for; it comes with what we call "on-the-job training." There are some things you won't learn in your practice room; it'll only come with being onstage or in the studio. A harsh reality is that it can feel different. From when you're in the practice room, to rehearsal, and to the stage, it can all be different. Adjust the best way you can and let your ears be your friend. It all comes down to hearing, retaining, and then applying.

Also, be mindful to pay special attention to how large the room is that you're playing in and adjust your intensity accordingly. Drums should not be a distraction—they should be a well-thought addition to any song.

Amassing vocabulary is again a deeply personal journey, just as is the application of that language. It's glaringly obvious, but in the main, you learn similar words to each other, but the sentences and phrases you construct; they are somewhat individual. Music is no different, it's a language, and a universal language at that.

As you can tell, my own journey led to me amassing a vocabulary initially through being immersed in a musical setting where I had to learn that language in order to be able to communicate. It becomes instinctive, and the ability to memorize is greatly improved through this approach.

There have been instances on my journey where I am subjected to new styles. And, as such I have had to learn elements of a new language—Latin-influenced music being a great example. I may not have grown up immersed in clave and cascara, but having acquired solid fundamentals through my own church-influenced upbringing, when I encountered these fresh approaches, it may have become just that much easier to first imitate, understand, and ultimately apply this new vocabulary.

Expanding my rhythmic vocabulary is equally as important to me as expanding my technique, and indeed, there are many instances of me having drum features where I may apply tension and release in those sections through the use of across-the-measure phrases, which delay the resolution back to beat 1 (Lady Gaga's performance of "Applause" at Coachella in 2017 is one such example), or through the displacement of the snare hit or backbeat. The more vocabulary you immerse yourself in, the more options you'll have at your disposal, and the more likely you are to create something unique.

Everyone will likely each memorize vocabulary through different means and stimuli: from records, from notation, from teachers, from videos, etc. Some will use a mixture of these means while others may prefer a single approach. The reality is that each and all may be fine as long as you ultimately apply what you learn *musically*. Experience has taught me that many great players will amass and understand vocabulary and concepts differently, but however I approach vocabulary, I can only apply it at a professional level if I have memorized and internalized it to a subconscious level, just as we all do with our native tongues.

Find the approaches which work best for you, but always keep an open mind—what works for you today may be somewhat different in the future, or it may change depending on the musical style or context you find yourself in. Above all though, always keep adding to your vocabulary, but always with a view to allow you to *create*, not just recreate.

As I have referred to, the genres I immersed myself in helped form my technique, as opposed to me using a genre as a vehicle to showcase a technique which I learned independently. It's an approach that has served me well and has allowed me to add value to artists from a diverse range of backgrounds and musical upbringings. However you choose to go about it, always work hard to develop your language and your technique as a means to express yourself and as a means to apply yourself to a variety of musical settings. Learning more vocabulary in the early stages of your development is vital.

One of the greatest compliments ever paid to me is around my versatility. In truth, I am always working to become more versatile, but the fact that I can adapt quickly to a variety of settings and contribute to the artist's and the musical director or producer's vision, with my own personal approach to the music, is hugely rewarding but is definitely a life-long journey. And the guys who stay in the business are often those who love the journey.

IMPROVISATION AND SOLOING

Both improvisation and soloing can take on different meanings, depending on the musical context you find yourself in. But regardless of the stylistic requirements, both can provide opportunities to express yourself and also to communicate with other improvising musicians and the audience. It's probably fair to say that both are an extension of the fundamentals I have discussed in previous chapters, and truly improvising can be difficult if you don't have: an accomplished sense of time, tone, and pulse; the ability to memorize and internalize form and structure; a genuine understanding of genre-specific conventions and vocabulary, or the technical facility necessary to relay your musical ideas.

That doesn't mean to say that you shouldn't be investigating improvisation or soloing as you develop these areas—you always should. Improvising and soloing can be a great way to develop your own ideas and also to internalize and apply many of the fundamental skills you have been working so hard to develop. But the options I have when improvising and soloing are greatly increased by the development of fundamentals, and it becomes a virtuous circle: the more the fundamentals improve, the more engaging, relevant, and interesting the improvisation or soloing becomes.

To truly improvise while being true to the groove and the context, adding tension and release through the use of rhythm, dynamics, and instrumentation, and communicating effortlessly with your bandmates can be one of the hallmarks of a truly accomplished musician. These factors can add to a performance in a way that any amount of preparation and rehearsal sometimes cannot.

One of the most time-honored questions around improvisation has always been, "Is it truly improvising if we are using vocabulary and rudiments?" I doubt there is a black or white answer to this, but my own approach has been simply to "be musical" in any context I find myself in. If I can respond musically and provide tension and release with complete control of my dynamics and tone, whether I am utilizing a technique or rudiment I have practiced previously, or applying a rhythmic concept which is already a part of my rhythmic vocabulary, is really irrelevant to me. The final effect on the group's performance and what we collectively relay to the audience is the true purpose, and how we get there can (and probably should) be unique to each of us.

I have performed in stadiums where I have a section in which to improvise or solo, and in those instances, I am not consciously contriving anything; I am merely just aiming to continue the musical conversation. Whether that is an exhibition of some technical mastery or of an advanced rhythmic approach, is incidental at that point. But the fact that I have practiced and memorized these techniques and concepts, plus a huge amount of music generally, has given me the best opportunity to add to that performance, at that time.

The things I have chosen to study have gone a long way to creating my own style. The way I choose to apply those will vary from artist to artist and show to show, but when I am performing at my best, I am not consciously thinking about what to include; I am letting it flow. Or as the sports psychologists and commentators often say, I am "in the zone." Just be sure to practice those fundamentals to the point where getting in the zone and creating unconsciously becomes a habit. To that end, a huge benefit and instant reward is to use some of your practice and rehearsal time to practice improvisation and soloing in order to train that part of your brain and also to apply those concepts and techniques which you have been working so hard to develop. It will be hugely beneficial and instantly rewarding.

It can be all too easy to lose sight of the importance of playing creatively while you are imitating the techniques and approaches of your idols, but there is a fair chance you have chosen to learn those approaches because of how *creative* the originators of those ideas were and not just based on the technical facility they possess. (Tony Williams can blow us all away while playing hardly anything technical, but the feel, sense of time, and his ability to play with the form—that's unique, whether it's as part of the accompaniment, or part of a solo.)

Just a quick note on form and intensity: It's best to look at soloing as a gradual build, very similar to how a song might build intensity through its form and structure. Take your time and paint a picture that tells everyone who you are through the drums (or any other instrument that you play). Start as simple and basic as you like, and after a while, add some more colors. Once we have the technical ability to truly express ourselves, improvisation and soloing can really show your musical personality.

There are some songs you may think are not solo-worthy, but then the artist asks you to solo. It's up to you how to approach this: Sometimes, it's just four bars at the end of a song or the entire eight bars of a section; at other points, everyone walks away off stage and lets you play for an extended period. Just like everything else, the more you do it, the better you become. Different time-feels, tempos, forms, and other factors may each determine your approach.

There's no right or wrong way to solo, but one great approach is to use a musical component of the song to enhance your solo. Create a foundation by using elements from the song or from the basic groove that's been established. You'll hear many jazz players talk about the melody of the song as being crucial as a reference point for soloing and improvisation, and you've heard me make reference to the lyrics and vocal melody earlier in the book. We need to know as many parts of the song as possible in order to do it justice: melody; chord progressions; form; samples; bass parts etc. How you use and interpret these elements will be unique and personal to you.

If there is an instance where you are starting the song with a solo, then always consider the song that you're about to play (it sounds obvious, but can be overlooked by aspiring students). This will give you a better overview of what you're attempting to execute, and help ensure relevance. Remember: Grooves, and groove development, can be a very effective tool in soloing. When I play, I aim to make everything groove, regardless of the context, and it provides a basis from which I can develop, add intensity, and ultimately paint that picture.

Here's part of the song "Chocolate," which appears in Part 3 of the book. The solo starts off with a lot of space, which then builds into increasingly complex figures and phrases. It's important to create variety for the listener to take in, so I used a mixture of melodic phrasing on the toms at the beginning and more groove-based figures later on that highlight the kit as a whole.

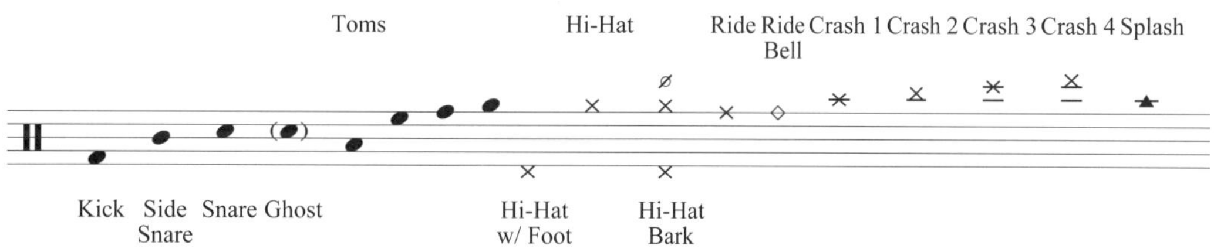

3
6
○

Back to side snare
mf

WORKING WITH BACKING TRACKS, SEQUENCERS, ELECTRONICS, AND PROGRAMMED PARTS

There are many things needed to play with backing tracks, but the two main components are timing and discipline, which are learned after you've mastered the fundamentals. You have to be a special person to play with backing tracks. There's a constant click going on in your ears, along with whatever is on the tracks. Depending on the gig, it could be less than others. Usually eight tracks will come from the playback engineer. Tracks 1-2 are usually drums, 3-4 are the other instruments, 5-6 are the vocals, and 7-8 are the click and slates. (Slates are count-offs for intros or accents; in the song; you'll hear a vocal count of "1-2-3-4.") The key for me is for the click to sit along with the tracks and not be overpowering in my ears. You can use the default sound, but my favorite sound is the cowbell. It's an actual instrument (as opposed to an artificial "beep"), and it will fit much better with the band sitting in your ears.

Sometimes, when you're playing to a click, and you are "locked," you will find that it actually disappears within the mix. If this has ever happened to you, then you'll know that it's kind of freaky. If you can hear it, then you may either be a little ahead or behind the beat. Don't panic! The reason I say discipline is the key is because there's a lot going on all at once. There are tours with crazy production where everything is locked to what they call the SMPTE, which is a timecode first created by the Society of Motion Picture and Television Engineers. (It's an annoying sound that links all audio, video content, and lights, all at the same time.)

We can't forget the electronics that are often added to the equation. In this case, the playback engineer will be your best friend. You can dissect the kicks, snare, and signature sounds from the actual stems (assuming the drums are separated). He/she will give me the stems on a USB drive, after which I'll upload them onto my machines, and then take the sound out of the box (a term used for playback). I usually use triggers as well and external pads with the same sounds that appear on the original recording. This creates more layers to produce a show that sounds amazing.

At this point, it's a given that you should already know the song and structure; discipline is the only thing that will get you through. Again, start with the kick and snare, playing those sounds out the box. Artists and MDs require you to completely recreate the album sounds (or as close you can). Between the electronics and acoustic drums, we have to find a way to mix the two together without creating a distraction within the song.

Playing parts is more than half of the battle, but there are other problems that we have to deal with. Some sounds require a clap sound with the snare, and some trigger systems will also affect the sound of the drum itself. The battle is trying not to get in the way of the tracks, as well as making each track feel organic, despite the amount of electronics.

Most MDs know exactly what they want to hear from you. All you have to do is interpret what they want. Some MDs are more passive and will see what you can come up with while some will let you do what you want. But even then, we still have to use discipline. In my head, I breakdown the parts into different sections. This can be note by note, bar by bar, four beats at a time or the amount of beats in that bar. In your own playing, take it from there until you get more comfortable and move on. Then, take it four bars at a time. You can then move on to eight bars, and even 16. (These types of phrases are harder to break down, but it's still possible.)

The placement of strokes is another thing that falls under discipline. You have to find a way to mix and master placing the strokes without ghost notes or crashes, often on beat 1. Don't play the hi-hat; just use the snare and kick. Depending on the song, you could be caught in any of these situations. Be ready to dumb down all of your musical vocabulary to play a simple part. It takes an incredible person to listen to a click all night, playing less than half of the information you've practiced in your garage or basement. However, when it all comes together, it's amazing.

WORKING WITH MUSICAL DIRECTORS, CHOIR MASTERS, DANCERS, PRODUCERS, AND ARTISTS

Young drummers that come out of the church are often branded as playing busy with too many notes. Well, I was right along with that trend but only for a few times before my mom (the director of the choir at my dad's church) got to me. I didn't have the freedom to play whatever I wanted as a drummer. She would shut me down as soon as I played something that had nothing to do with the song. She told me, "You are playing with us, not the other way around. The band is to be an accompaniment, not a distraction." These words will always stick with me because it's so true.

Working with choir directors is always fun; most of them are just like MDs. There are some things you can get away with. Church is a great place to learn how to adjust on the fly, figuring out exactly what's needed in your playing. My mom wasn't too passive, but she did allow us to express ourselves. Directors will often start a song in one tempo, and when they realize it's too slow, they'll look over to the drummer, making gestures to speed the song up until it's at the tempo that they feel is correct. It's a lot like a conductor for an orchestra. They can decide to start on the bridge, or they can break the music down to just the vocals. Learning to move on the fly is a crash course in churches across the world. It's a bit extreme, but it ultimately improves your learning.

When we sat down to play in church, we had to be ready and attentive. The pastor could get up at any time and start singing a song that he felt in his heart. They would often start in a random key, so the organist (a dominant instrument in black churches) would have to find the key that he/she was singing in, and it was off to the races at that point! We all would join in as if we started the song off ourselves. I had to be able to do these things throughout my childhood, so after many years playing under those conditions, it was fairly easy for me to merge into the pop and R&B world. My instincts would kick in, even with managing the drumset while playing.

Growing up, our church didn't have the best gear. Sometimes, the cymbal stand would fall to a lower height while you were playing. Every time I hit that cymbal, it would get lower and lower. I would put one stick down while playing and fix the stand. Then, I would pick up the other stick and continue playing as if nothing happened.

During my first major gig with a mainstream artist, I had a drum tech who would assist me, yet a similar thing happened to me in one show that regularly happened to me in church as a child. The cymbal stand was getting lower and lower every time I hit the cymbal. I put one stick down, continued playing, and fixed the cymbal stand before my tech even knew what happened. I got in a little trouble that day; he said, "Let me do my job; I got you." It was just like second nature for me to do it.

We have to take on that mentality on the stage or wherever we're playing. You have to be comfortable enough with your drums (or any other instrument) that no matter what happens, you can be quick on your feet and not be a distraction. Now, don't get me wrong—we all deal with things that go wrong, and we can't react that fast. However, in most cases, we are in control over ourselves and nothing else. Human error is going to happen.

PART 2: SOLO POP DRUM EXAMPLES

HAVANA

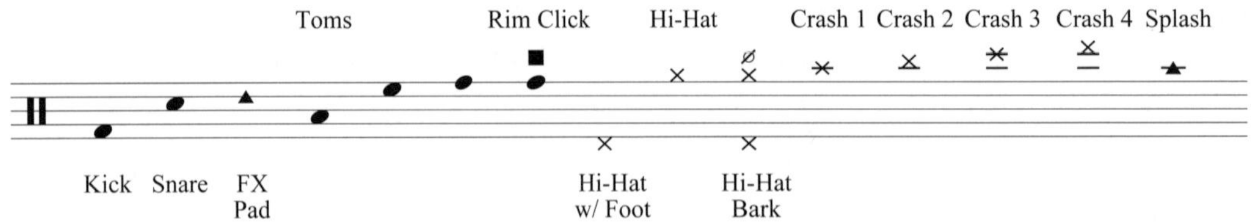

C
mf
f
D
mf
E
f
F
6
6
mf

f
mf
f
G
mf
f
H

NOTES ABOUT THE SONG:

In Camila Cabello's song, "Havana," it's important for me to remain in the spirit of the tune. I remember the first time I heard this song; it was the first day of rehearsal. I believe we had one week to put an entire show together including this song and several others. I had just come off another tour at that moment and needed to get things deleted from my head so I could get more music into my brain. It was great songwriting along with an amazing vocalist, so my responsibility to this was to be as respectful to the music as possible. The main backbeat of the song is an electric clap; there is no real snare drum played until the special parts. The kick pattern is dead-on to the song in its original form, and we try to remain true to the song unless there are some live additions to it. This song was arranged with a little touch of a Latin feel, so in the middle section—the dance break—we play a salsa groove. I'm playing cascara with my left hand (hi-hat hand) and clave with my right hand (snare hand). I had to learn this salsa groove with Jennifer Lopez a few years earlier, so it was cool to develop it further.

Click tracks and slates also help with knowing what comes up next. Some gigs and tours use slates and some use charts, while others require you to simply know the arrangement by heart. By the 50th show of the tour, you can imagine what the arrangement will sound like. We all would love to just make it a new experience every time we play a song, but it is best to keep it locked in and not get too crazy.

I WISH

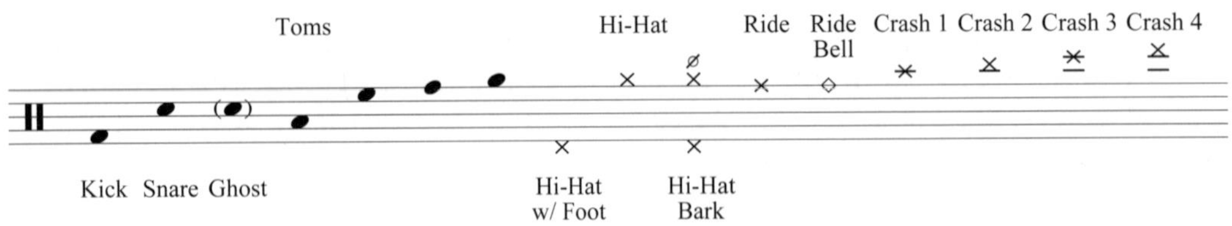
Toms
Hi-Hat
Ride
Ride Bell
Crash 1
Crash 2
Crash 3
Crash 4
Kick
Snare
Ghost
Hi-Hat w/ Foot
Hi-Hat Bark

♩ = 103
mf
A
f
mf

B
sim.
C
6

D
mf
E
3
3

F

NOTES ABOUT THE SONG:

This song reminds me of the first time I played with Stevie Wonder. When I first met Stevie, I was 25 years old. It was in New York City, and I'll never forget it. Teddy Campbell called me, saying that he had to get back to LA, so I took over for him. While I was setting up the drums and getting comfortable, Stevie walked in. I was super nervous and scared at this point, especially knowing who he is and all his accomplishments. I found myself totally starstruck and completely set back as to what was happening.

He didn't speak to anyone; instead, he walked straight to the piano and started playing John Coltrane's "Giant Steps." Then, everyone started following him, including me. We played for about 20 minutes; everyone took a solo and it was so much fun! This helped to make me comfortable and honored to be in the room with some true musical giants. We ended the song, and Stevie said, "Let's take a break." I felt much better after playing with him, so during the break, I went to the piano and introduced myself. In our conversation, he said to me "Just be yourself and loosen up a bit." He was super cool—I felt like I was dreaming!

Stevie's monumental song, "I Wish," deserves all the respect that it is due. One of Stevie's biggest hits to date, I always hear the song played on the radio, in jam sessions, etc. Playing the song with Stevie and the band was totally different than only listening to it in its original form. I had to approach playing this song with the arrangement that was on Stevie's live album *Natural Wonder*. The first thing I had to learn was the correct kick pattern. With a song like this, you think it's played one way, but in fact, it's totally different. I was corrected on that in the very first rehearsal. With all the nervousness involved, I had to be sure to get it right. Once I did, it was amazing how each part and pattern came together. What was most important for me to remember while playing this song was to keep the timing consistent, making the groove more exciting. I knew when I was correctly playing because his feet would be tapping away.

If you ever find yourself playing behind Stevie on this song, just watch his feet—they will never steer you wrong!

YOU ARE THE SUNSHINE OF MY LIFE

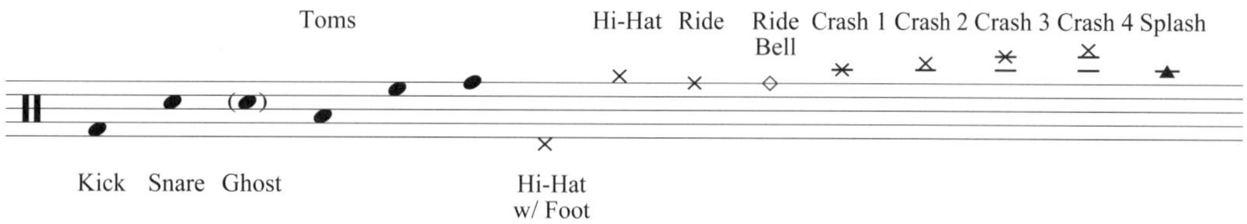

B
f
C
mf

D
Loosen hi-hats
f
sim.
3
rubato

NOTES ABOUT THE SONG:

"You Are the Sunshine of My Life" takes slightly more finesse than some of the other tunes I play with Stevie. The most dynamic song in the set, it features cross sticking techniques and a bossa nova groove for the verses. As the song increases dynamically, move to the ride cymbal to enhance the energy, all while still maintaining the cross-sticking. Once that sequence is over, then the snare comes in, almost like a double time feel into the ending. It's hugely important to recognize how to get into the big ending. You only get about a bar to set up the ending, so it absolutely must count. The first hit is accented on the "and" of beat 4, so the placement of the fill is crucial. If it's too soon, then it's out of place; if it's too late, then you've missed your chance to nail the setup. However, there's nothing like adding a little flavor to an iconic song and arrangement.

SUPERSTITION

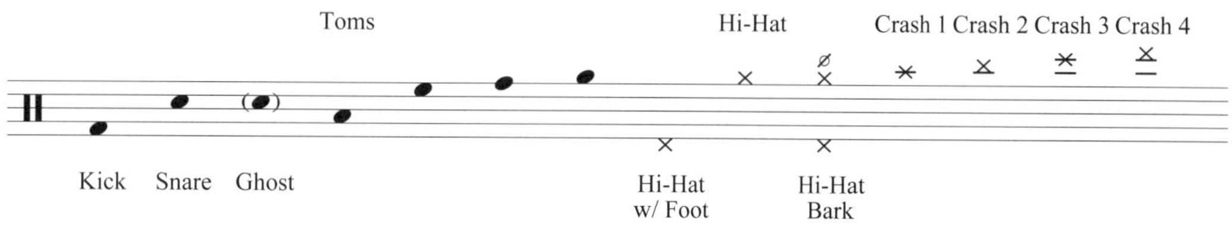

f
B
6
C
mf
f

After you gain a deeper awareness of many styles, you will find that most of these beats and grooves are related to each other. It's more about the approach and variety of sounds that sets each genre apart. Pay attention to the swing of the groove; some styles require fewer notes than others. Pulling back the number of notes will help ensure that your ears are open to listen to the parts around you and the overall feel, before getting to the core of the groove. Even ballads—the simplest of grooves—will get you on the right track for developing skills in using dynamics and intensity in your playing. Use mallets and play cymbal swells to take the place of classical orchestration in the song. To get different articulations, you can use brushes. Most of all, use space, as drums can be very impactful and loud. Surprise yourself by adding your own color and patterns to the song. Like creating a painting, be free to enjoy the journey of the musical style.

D

E

NOTES ABOUT THE SONG:

This is a great song that's played at every jam session in the world and beyond. It initially sounds simple, but it's more complex despite how simple it seems on the surface. It starts with drums, using a four-on-the-floor kick drum, 2 + 4 backbeat on the snare, and swinging hi-hats that provide the dominating force throughout the song and give it its signature character. In the first B section of the song, there is a specific fill that Stevie asked me to play in rehearsal, and it's what I've always played since.

Stevie's a genius, and I respect that about him. He still wants the song to be true to the performance and not limited to how he heard the song or interpretation. The iconic intro of "Superstition" is such a huge thing—it sets the tone for the rest of the song. Playing the intro correctly is half the battle.

JUST DANCE

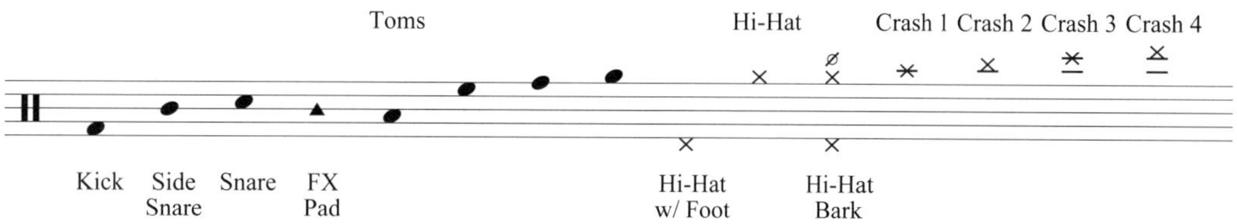
Toms
Hi-Hat
Crash 1 Crash 2 Crash 3 Crash 4
Kick
Side Snare
Snare
FX Pad
Hi-Hat w/ Foot
Hi-Hat Bark

♩ = 120
f
A
mf
B
f

C
p
mf
3
D
f
mf

E
f
mf
F
f

NOTES ABOUT THE SONG:

This song by Lady Gaga represents pop music at its finest. At the end of 2016, I received a call from my long-time friend and brother, Tim Stewart. The conversation went like this: "Hey bro, what's up? Are you busy this January and February? You wanna do the Super Bowl with Lady Gaga?" That was the call I was looking for. The first days into 2017 found me in a room with a bunch of strangers, entirely in a whole new world. I knew Tim and a few of the crew members, but again, I was getting into a gig where I felt slightly isolated. I made myself comfortable by approaching this rehearsal like I had with others before.

On the second day of rehearsal, Gaga walked in. She walked over to me, and I introduced myself. She was sweet and welcoming in return. She told me that I had a good energy and was happy that I could be there. That day, the set list for the Super Bowl had to be nailed down, but she couldn't decide which songs would work best for the performance. She approached me and said, "Chris, what do you think?" I replied, "Just Dance." She asked me, "Why?" and I said, "It's your first hit; you have to do this one." She walked away in true Gaga style and said, "OK." I'll never be sure if that song was inserted in the set because of my input, but the fact that she asked me only minutes after first meeting her was cool. She was comfortable, so that made me comfortable in return.

I have had the honor of playing this song on some of the biggest stages around the world. The song is a smash hit, so I always approach it with respect. Granted, by the time I started playing with her, the song had evolved through a few phases, resulting in being played with a little more edge. Live drums replace the recorded, programmed sounds throughout the song, adding a little hi-hat on the second half of the verse and open hi-hats on the chorus. Despite the prominent rock element that's now included, it's still best to keep to the recorded patterns and play with as much of the original feel as possible.

All these things considered, having fun with preparation can take you places as a player that you've only dreamed of. Working with Gaga is easy; I play what's required in the song. I always start with the basis of the groove and build it from there, incorporating elements from the kit and other devices. Electronic components are always going to be a requirement now. This occurs mainly in the bridge of "Just Dance," using a specific clap sound, and then it goes back to the live groove. It's important to make each section of the song feel the same, keeping the same intensity throughout. Whether the sounds are electronic or live, the audience shouldn't be able to tell the difference between sections.

APPLAUSE

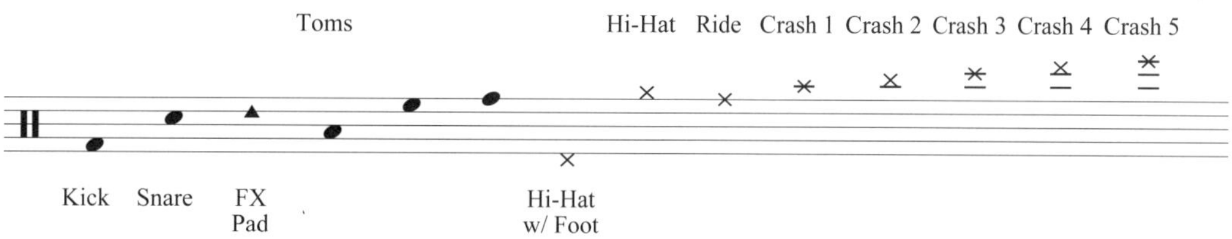
Toms
Hi-Hat
Ride
Crash 1
Crash 2
Crash 3
Crash 4
Crash 5
Kick
Snare
FX Pad
Hi-Hat w/ Foot

♩ = 140
f
mf
f
3

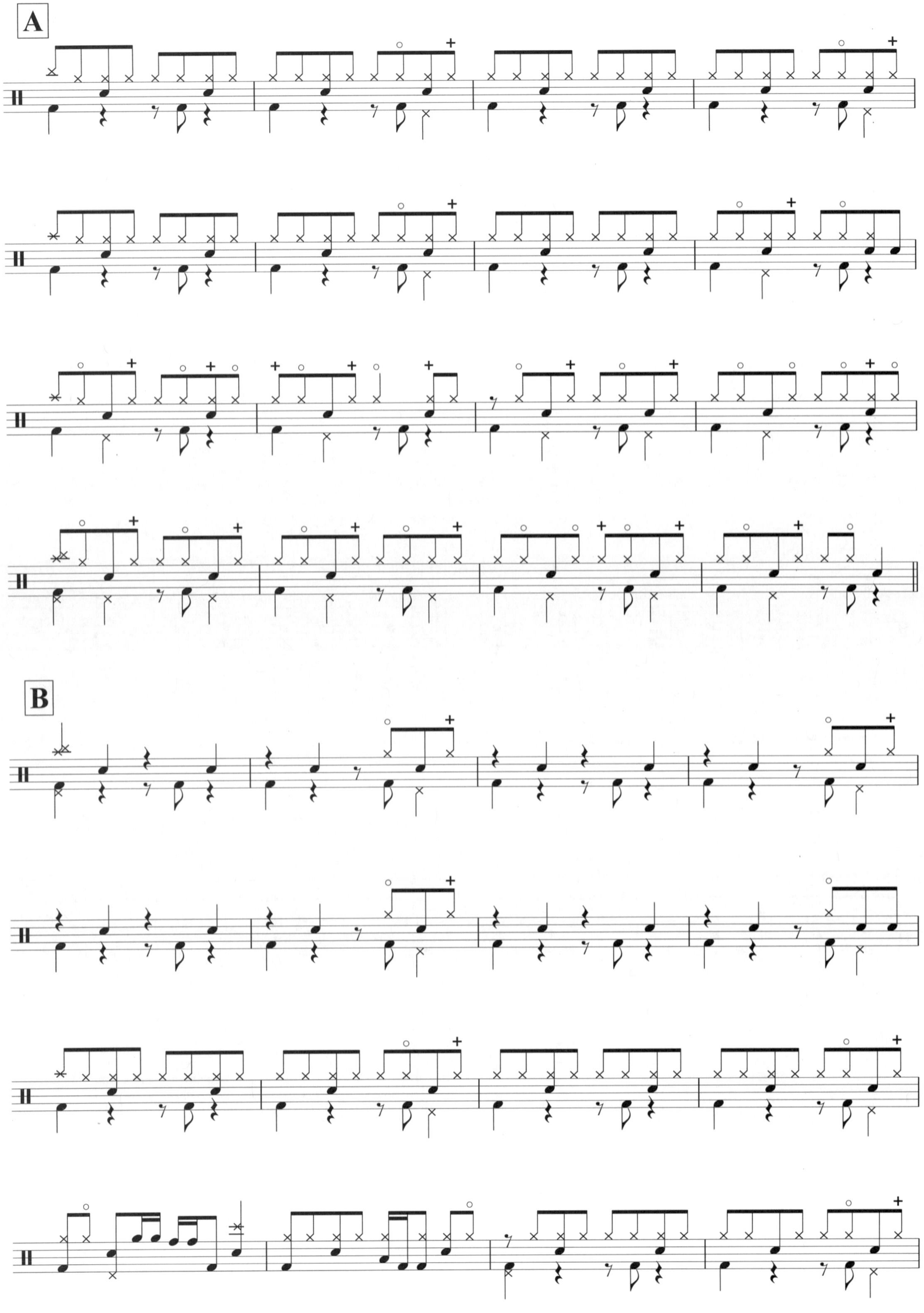
A
B

mf
f
C
D
mf
f

mf
E
f
Loosen hi-hats

NOTES ABOUT THE SONG:

This is one of my favorite songs from Gaga to play in the setlist. After playing it at the Super Bowl, we took it to Coachella. This song had been arranged into a few different versions, so we rehearsed and perfected all three until one was chosen. I was filled with excitement while getting ready for the soundcheck for Coachella. It was my first time playing there, and I couldn't wait to play. It was early in the morning, so hardly anybody on the fairgrounds. This is the first song to use for the soundcheck, and for some reason, my sound was the best I've ever heard it. Everything was just right, which fueled my excitement leading up to showtime.

Now, it's time to play! The kick drum and snare drive this song. That sounds simple, right? After the entrance of the kick drum and snare, the hi-hat pattern is added, keeping the drive of the initial groove going. What separates the verse and chorus is playing four-on-the-floor into an electric snare fill for a huge climax into the chorus. After the second chorus, there's a huge band moment, allowing for a sort of mini drum solo to take place. Each time I play this, I keep in mind that the rest of the band is helping me, so I can't go too crazy. Showcasing the band in this song is the best because of the dynamic chorus and ending. After all, it's a rock show with Lady Gaga! Playing the groove of this song has its challenges, especially when keeping the kick drum and snare consistent to drive the song forward.

UMBRELLA

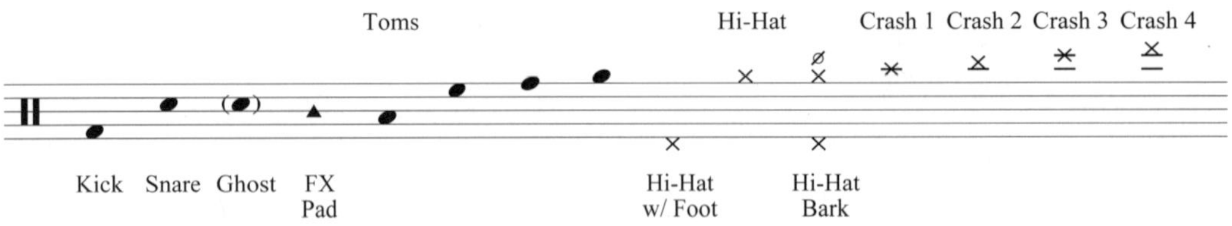
Toms
Hi-Hat
Crash 1
Crash 2
Crash 3
Crash 4
Kick
Snare
Ghost
FX Pad
Hi-Hat w/ Foot
Hi-Hat Bark

♩ = 86
mf
f
A
mf

B
f
mf
C
3
f
D

E
mf
f
F
6
6

NOTES ABOUT THE SONG:

I've had the pleasure of playing this iconic song by Rihanna for more than six years, including five tours, countless festivals, and variety shows. Turn back time to circa 2006; at this point, every musician wanted to be on the legendary Jay Leno television show. In LA, you were considered to have "made it" if you appeared on Jay Leno, and this performance was one of my best memories with her. Rihanna was a new, young artist, but everyone saw the potential of how successful she could become. Her success would be virtually guaranteed if that television performance went well. It did, and the rest, they say, is history.

It was a fun challenge to recreate a drum sample and then play this song all over the world, three times over. Like many of the other recordings so far, this groove starts the song, so the pressure can feel high. The original groove is made up of highly detailed and specifically placed samples, so the opening and cut-offs of the hi-hat cymbals are vital. Playing this song live means that you must recreate the track note-for-note, so you must be spot on. The song starts with a verse from Jay-Z, and the hip-hop groove takes over. In hip-hop drumming, you usually play along with the recorded track, so you must blend well with it. In any case, the correct sounds and grooves are the focus, but with this song, it's especially important.

PART 3: FULL BAND EXAMPLES

PARTY

Written by Chris Johnson, John "Jubu" Smith, and Nate Watts

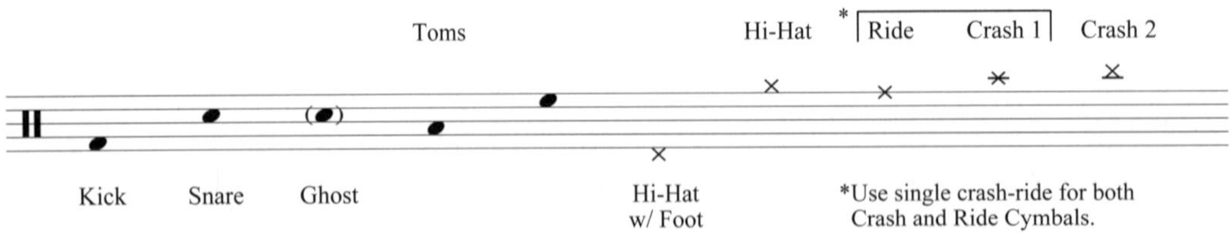

B

C

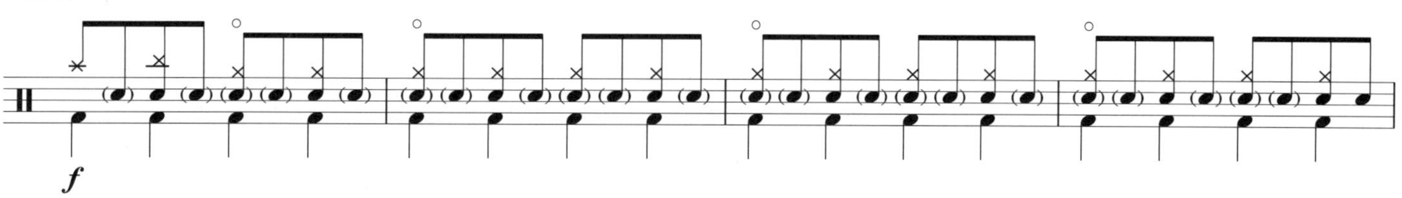

mf
f

D
mf
f
mf

E
f
mf
f
mf
F
f
ritardando
Go crazy!
ff

NOTES ABOUT THE SONG:

Nate Watts - Bass

John "Jubu" Smith - Guitar

While working with Stevie Wonder, I had the honor of playing with the legendary bassist Nate Watts, who has been at Stevie's side for over 40 years. Nate is as old-school as you can get, and he has taught me so much about how to approach music. It was only right to have him as a part of this session.

We wanted to take an old-school approach to a traditional shuffle. I played a more jazz-based kit for "Party." With the shuffle technique, I've patterned my approach after a few drummers I've seen; one in particular is Bernard Purdie. I've never had the chance to sit in with Bernard, but he's a big influence, so I have often applied his approach when practicing the things that I find stylistically relevant. In truth, this is done probably more instinctively than consciously, but I can always hear and feel Bernard's influence.

Technique-wise, this one predominantly features heel-up on the kick drum and matched grip on the sticks. Playing a shuffle requires me to use my left hand on my snare and my right hand on the hi-hat or crash/ride cymbal—yes, we "lefties" aren't always strictly open-handed!

On this song, my jazz-oriented kit features a 20″ kick, 13″ rack tom, 16″ floor tom, 22″ crash, and 22″ crash-ride. Sonically, I wanted to make it feel and sound like real, old-school R&B.

FORGET ABOUT YOU

Written by John "Jubu" Smith and Harold Lilly

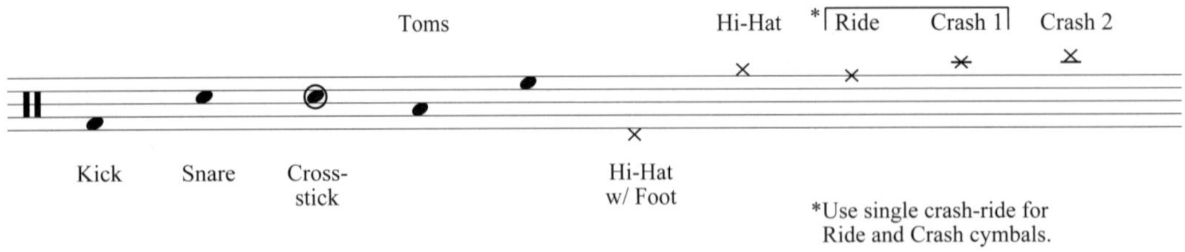

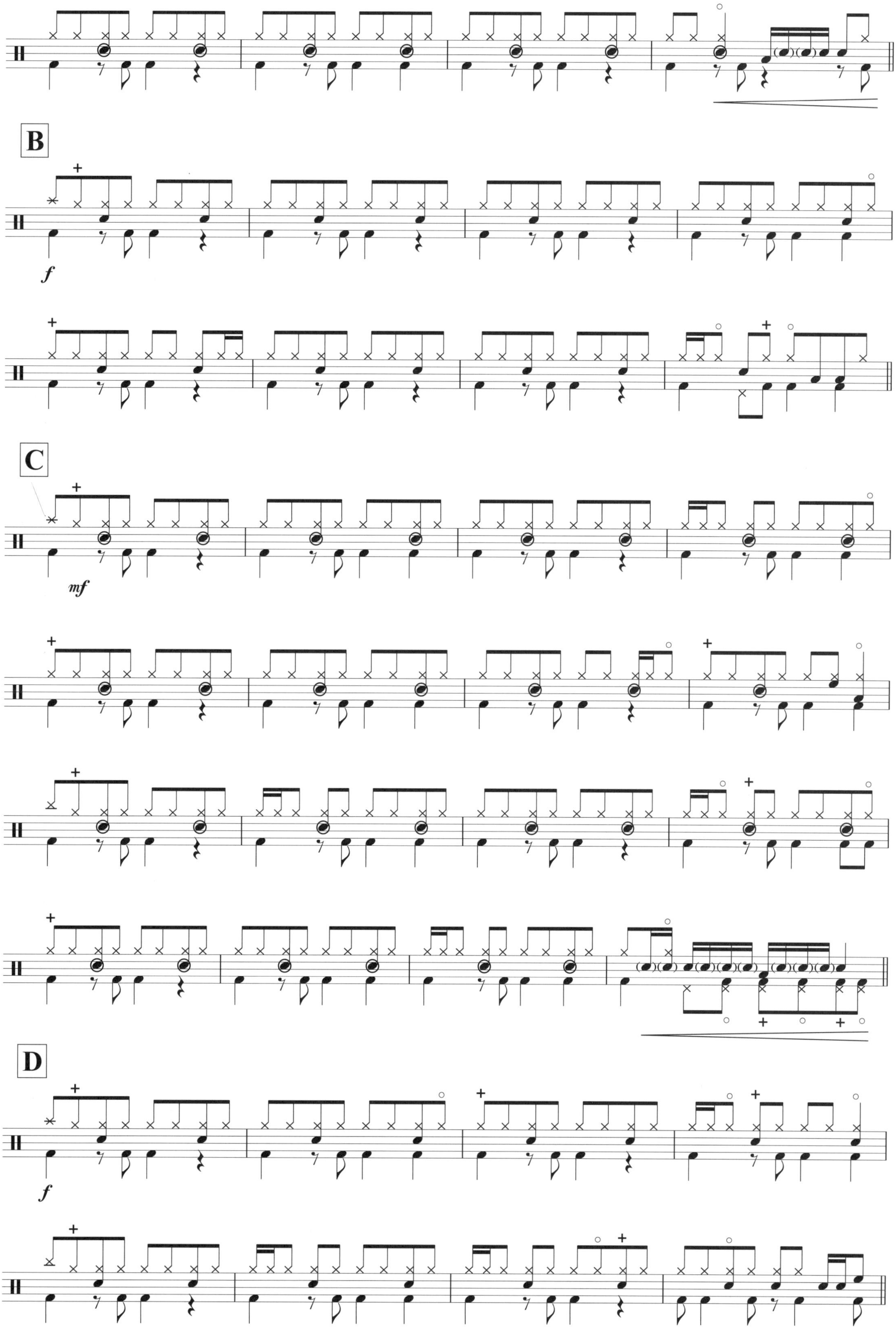
B
f
C
mf
D
f

E
mf
F

G
f
H
I

J
ff
f
molto ritardando

WHY BREAK MINE

Written by John "Jubu" Smith and Ledesi

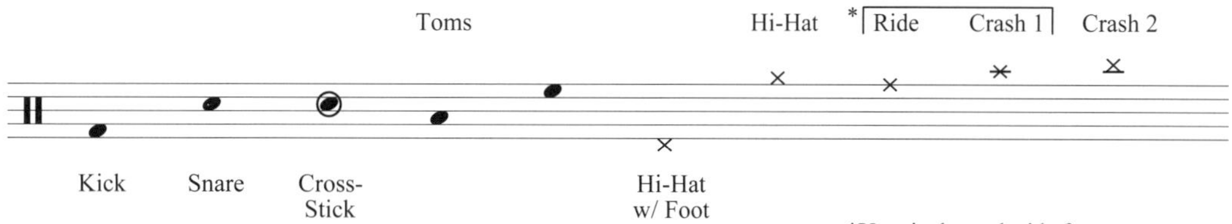

*Use single crash-ride for Ride and Crash cymbals.

B

C
mf
mf
mf

mf
D
f
E
mf

F

G
mf
2
f
rubato

NOTES ABOUT THE SONGS:

Legally Blynd

John "Jubu" Smith - Guitar

Eric Smith - Bass

Errol Cooney - Guitar

Bennett Paysinger - Hammond B3 Organ

Michael Bereal - Fender Rhodes

You can find "Forget About You" on our self-titled, debut album *Legally Blynd*. These songs have a more contemporary sound, but they're still groove-based and a part of the R&B genre. The guitar solo is played by Errol Cooney, who I have been fortunate to play with extensively in Stevie's band. This track is relatively straightforward in terms of form and structure, but as always, time, feel, tone production, and dynamic control are the areas to pay most attention to.

"Why Break Mine" is featured on Legally Blynd's latest album entitled *You*. This track is more complex, and you could either interpret it as being in 4/4 with triplets as the overriding subdivisions, or in 6/8 time (with elements of an Afro Cuban 6/8 shared amongst the band), using eighth notes as the subdivision. This track features a great, two-guitar arrangement that really showcases the all-around musicianship of Eric and Jubu; it really captures their feel, dynamics, time, tone, and aural skills. This is one of my favorites to play—there are highs and lows, textures, colors, and tension and release—it's all in there.

These are relatively simple parts, but paying attention to the time-feel is crucial. You should still use matched grip and heel up, always relaxed.

My setup is fairly simple for these songs; there aren't too many equipment combinations that are used. The kit for these songs consists of a 20″ kick, 13″ rack tom, 16″ floor tom, 22″ crash, and a 22″ crash-ride.

GET AWAY

Written by Carl Wheeler, Chris Johnson, Eric Smith, Errol Cooney, and John "Jubu" Smith

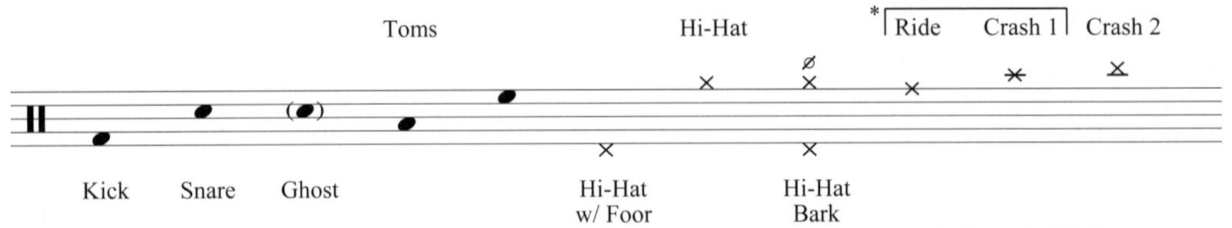

*Use single crash-ride for Ride and Crash cymbals.

B

f
C
mf

f
mf
f
mf
f
D
mf

f
mf

E
f

NOTES ABOUT THE SONG:

Legally Blynd

John "Jubu" Smith - Guitar

Eric Smith - Bass

Errol Cooney - Guitar

Bennett Paysinger - Hammond B3 Organ

Michael Bereal - Fender Rhodes

"Get Away" is a previously unreleased song that is largely improvisatory and also somewhat of a drum feature. The intro is quite indicative of my approach when I get some space to stretch out on groove-based gigs, as is the drum section later in the track. I often use some elements of displacement and across-the-bar phrasing to help provide tension and release in the music. For instance, I have been on stadium gigs with Lady Gaga where this approach has allowed me to provide more interest to sections where I'm featured but without losing the pulse, groove, and feel for the whole stadium.

This track features a great loop with so many places to showcase musicianship and have a little fun. It's also a great song to work on timing and different combinations of improvised fills and chops. The kit that I used for this track consists of a 20" kick, 13" rack tom, 16" floor tom, 22" crash, and a 22" crash-ride.

HOLY, HOLY, HOLY

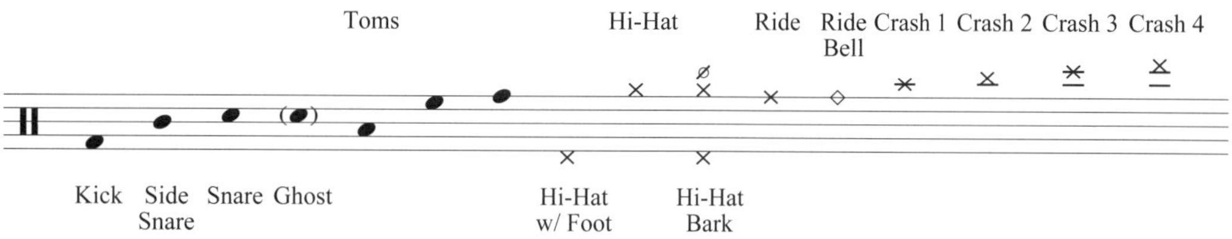

f
mf
B
f
mf

C
f
D
mf

f
mf

NOTES ABOUT THE SONG:

Micheal Bereal - Piano

Bennett Paysinger - Hammond B3 Organ

Bryan "B-Dub" White - Bass

John "Jubu" Smith - Guitar

"Holy, Holy, Holy" is one of my favorite hymns to sing in church. Growing up in church, I wanted to share some of my musical roots by merging the traditional with the new. The original song does not have an upbeat feel to it like this arrangement. I wanted to create a feel-good beat while keeping it simple. I have never underestimated the importance of groove, and it incorporates most of the fundamentals which have served me so well: touch, control, internal dynamics, time, and listening. Here, I am consistently laying down the backbeat on beats 2 and 4 while leaving the guys and the chord changes in the forefront. However, some of the hi-hat figures may prove a handy workout for you.

A lot of the "pop" sounds you hear nowadays come out of the church tradition, and it has been a discipline I am ever thankful for being introduced to.

The cymbals I used for this song included a 22″ ride and crashes sizes ranging from 20″ to 22″ and 19″. The hi-hat size was 16″; it creates a nice universal sound for the styles we've covered in this book. The drums that I used were 8″, 10″, and 12″ rack toms and a 16″ floor tom along with a mid-tone snare.

Church music is always high-energy, so I often adopt a slightly tighter grip on the sticks and implement both heel-up and heel-down techniques on the kick drum.

BUMP

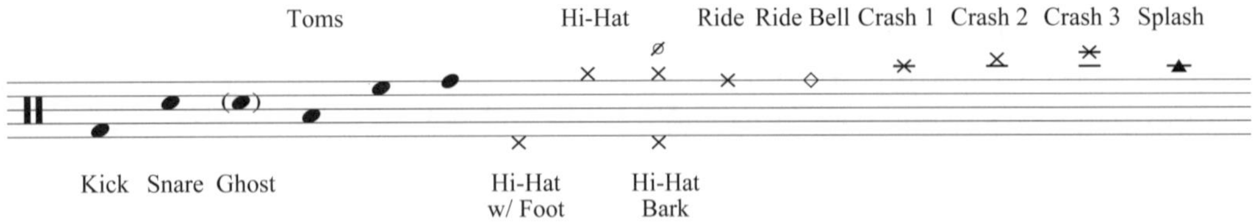
Toms
Hi-Hat
Ride
Ride Bell
Crash 1
Crash 2
Crash 3
Splash
Kick
Snare
Ghost
Hi-Hat w/ Foot
Hi-Hat Bark

♩ = 146
f
mf

A
f
B

C
mf
f

D
mf
f
sim.
E
mf
f

F
mf
f

NOTES ABOUT THE SONG:

Micheal Bereal - Piano

Bennett Paysinger - Hammond B3 Organ

Bryan "B-Dub" White - Bass

John "Jubu" Smith - Guitar

When you think of the Pentecostal church, you have to imagine hand-clapping, foot-stomping, tambourines, dancing around the church, and obviously praising God! "Bump" has it all. It features double-time and half-time feels, walking bass, **montuno** piano sections, a drum outro over a vamp, and a groove that takes a lot of energy, technique, and stamina to play. In church, this happens at the most random times, and it could be at any moment. The BPM is usually around 160 or above. It has a simple 2-and-4 beat and a high-rated BPM full of 16th- and 32nd-note combinations. The drum loop playing with the electronic percussion elements was a later addition to the church in playing "shouting music." It also helps to keep the beat constant and allowing for more improvisation. It takes a major amount of discipline to keep the groove going for the sake of the rest of the band and people shouting. For me, one of the most inspirational drummers in this type of setting is Joel Smith. He is super precise and distinct—a drummer to check out if you haven't already.

This track is a pretty tough workout, but this type of tempo is an essential part of the gospel music tradition. I use the heel-up technique on the kick to give me an advantage for all the advanced rhythm sections of the song. As always, I use a matched grip to play the drums, which consist of 8", 10", and 12" rack toms and a 16" floor tom along with a mid-tone snare. The cymbals include a 22" ride and crash sizes ranging from 20" to 22" and 19".

CHOCOLATE

Written by Chris Johnson, Courtney Leonard, Kamil Rustam, and Tim Carmon

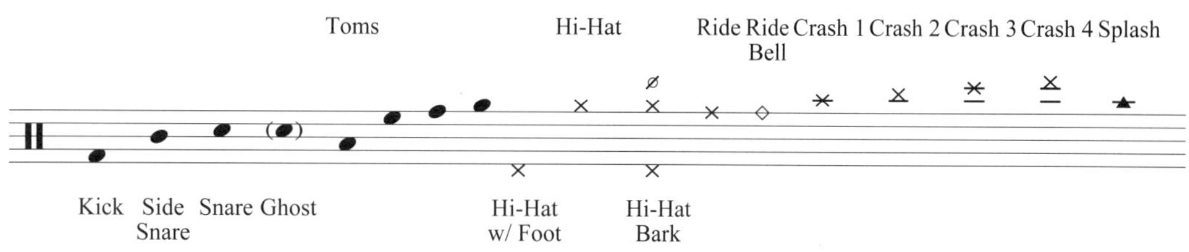

B
mp
mf

C
p
D
mp

mf
E
Switch to main snare
f

3
3
3
3
3
3
3
3
3
3
3
3
3
3
3
3

Back to side snare
mf
F

Switch to main snare
G
f

H
p

mp

NOTES ABOUT THE SONG:

Tim Carmon - Hammond B3 Organ and Fender Rhodes

Courtney Leonard - Bass

Kamil Rustam - Guitar

We really got to stretch out on this track, which has a similar feel to the song "I Feel Good." It features displaced snare rhythms, challenging hi-hat work, a solo section, a guitar solo, and is generally improvisatory in nature.

This kind of interplay tests some different skills within a fundamental, groove-based approach which is so essential for most contemporary pop settings. It reminds me that I'm blessed to spend my time performing with such high-level improvisers. There is a lot of complex content in this track, but my advice is to first approach it aurally and then read and analyze the notation. Reading is a brilliant skill and having notation to analyze is hugely beneficial. However, training our ears in much the same way we learned to speak our native language has been my most favored approach to learning. But, as with most things, we each have to find an individual approach which works for us personally.

The solo section is played on the mid-tone snare. Then, it goes back into the groove of the song on the lower-tone snare. The drums on this track include 8″, 10″, and 12″ rack toms and a 16″ floor tom. The cymbals include a 22″ ride and crash sizes ranging from 20″ to 22″ and 19″.

GROUP SONG

Written by Chris Johnson, Courtney Leonard, Kamil Rustam, and Tim Carmon

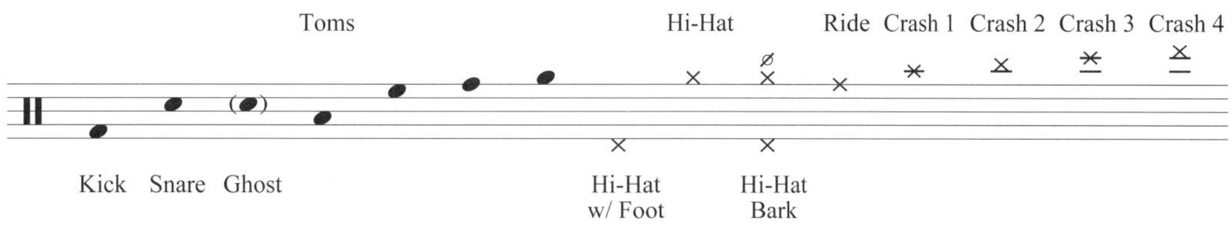

B
f
mf
f
mf
C
D

f
mf
E
f
mf
f
F
mf

G

NOTES ABOUT THE SONG:

Tim Carmon - Hammond B3 Organ and Fender Rhodes

Courtney Leonard - Bass

Kamil Rustam - Guitar

This song is one of the most pop-oriented from this session, incorporating a swing feel with a few electronic elements as well. The kick drum is mostly four-on-the-floor, keeping it simple but still funky. This allows me to enjoy the other elements in the band to create a simple, driving groove. This song is stylistically indicative of much of the repertoire and skills needed for the working professional contemporary pop drummer. Hopefully, there is not much included other than what is required to get people to dance!

This set-up is very similar to the ones I use for gospel and pop. I play the kick drum with a heel-up technique, a matched grip with the sticks, and I largely concentrate on nailing the groove. You can hear great interplay among the band with a mixture of repeating grooves and improvised sections.

The drums on this track include 8″, 10″, and 12″ rack toms and a 16″ floor tom along with a mid-tone snare. My cymbal selection is more or less suitable for a neutral sound. The cymbals include a 22″ ride and crash sizes ranging from 20″ to 22″ and 19″.

EPILOGUE: LIFE TIPS FOR MUSICIANS

Be a musician more than a drummer (this can apply to whichever instrument you play). Become any and everything given to you. Learn music that you've never thought of playing or listening to. The bigger your vocabulary, the more you can play and adapt to whatever is thrown at you. One particular groove or rhythm instantly connects with you, and you become whatever that genre is—it's like second nature to play the appropriate thing to seal in the authenticity of the groove within the music. Sounds and sizes of drums have a huge impact in how a groove is played. For example, if you sit down on a traditionally tuned jazz kit, then you might find that it'll take you to an instant bebop way of playing. All these elements work together to enable you to become as versatile as you can be in every genre and being able to play whatever is in front of you.

Playing with a band is like a car; where would the car be if there were no wheels? What if you have wheels but no engine, or a working engine but no frame? The point is that we each have a specific, crucial part to play in a band, and if we can just play our part for the bigger picture, then each band member would feel the group is reaching its full potential.

The physical aspects of playing the kit are essential. You need to be in control of your hands in order to control the drums. Hand stretches and warm ups are also crucial. But, in equal importance compared to physical control, mental and emotional control is absolutely necessary. Being in control of your mind allows you to be in control of the drums or whichever instrument you play. Being in control of your emotions and soul is being in control of your mindset and purpose. I've had to learn over the years that just playing drums is only a vehicle that will allow my true purpose to shine through. I believe an honest walk in life will help shape who you are as a musician. Maintain a level of professionalism that will allow people to be drawn to you, and be a light in all the madness to help bring a sense of calm over you and everyone that touches you. Apply this to artists, their management, MDs, bandmates, audio, lights, the guy taking the tickets at the door, and even the person that's cleaning the tables at the bar where you play. It's always good to maintain respect for yourself and represent yourself well.

All of these things are a factor in how we live our daily life, so that when we play our instrument, all we have to focus on is executing the task at hand. Being prepared will also help develop your technique; knowing what you have to do will help. With some gigs, we get the music ahead of time; this is when I will sit with the music until I know it as if I've been playing that particular gig my whole life. If there are any electronics, then I make sure that each sound is programmed and ready to go. On certain gigs, I don't play splashes while other gigs require them, so I adjust accordingly. On some gigs, there are no tracks, so you have to know tempos, and make sure all parts are covered. Some gigs may have all these factors present in one situation. If you know what the gig or show calls for, then you can adjust accordingly. Twenty years of on-the-job training has conditioned me and helped shape the player I am today.

Even at the intermediate and advanced playing, I still have to rely on timing. Without good timing, it is very hard to execute any kind of drum rolls or fills within a groove. What helps me the most in the practice room is repetition. The more you play, the more comfortable you will feel. The first place to start when getting comfortable starts with setting up the drums. It's all different for many, but when you sit at the drums, you have to be comfortable. Each factor makes a difference—the height of the snare, toms, and cymbals determines if you're hitting the sweet spot. Take the time to get all things in order so that you won't have to do so when it's time to play. Don't get me wrong—there will be times that you don't feel comfortable, so just do the best you can. If you're in control of how things go on gigs, then there should be plenty of time to prepare.

There are some instances where we just have to hop on and play. This happens in jam sessions and gigs where you have to share gear with someone else. This is where what I said about hand control earlier comes into play. If you can see the drum and identify where it is, then it's almost like golf. Your longest distance with a 9-iron is 145 yards. If the pin is only 138 yards, then you have to control the distance. It's hard and difficult at most times. I've had my fair share of missing the sweet spot on the drum or hitting the rim and not making good contact, but over the years, it becomes like second nature to hit the sweet spot. Practice and actually playing are the best teachers in all these instances. My greatest moments as a drummer were learning how to overcome certain obstacles and adjusting to what was given to me.

YOU CAN'T BEAT OUR DRUM BOOKS!

Bass Drum Control

Best Seller for More Than 50 Years!

by Colin Bailey

This perennial favorite among drummers helps players develop their bass drum technique and increase their flexibility through the mastery of exercises.

06620020 Book/Online Audio $17.99

The Complete Drumset Rudiments

by Peter Magadini

Use your imagination to incorporate these rudimental etudes into new patterns that you can apply to the drumset or tom toms as you develop your hand technique with the Snare Drum Rudiments, your hand and foot technique with the Drumset Rudiments and your polyrhythmic technique with the Polyrhythm Rudiments. Adopt them all into your own creative expressions based on ideas you come up with while practicing.

06620016 Book/CD Pack $14.95

Drum Aerobics

by Andy Ziker

A 52-week, one-exercise-per-day workout program for developing, improving, and maintaining drum technique. Players of all levels – beginners to advanced – will increase their speed, coordination, dexterity and accuracy. The online audio contains all 365 workout licks, plus play-along grooves in styles including rock, blues, jazz, heavy metal, reggae, funk, calypso, bossa nova, march, mambo, New Orleans 2nd Line, and lots more!

06620137 Book/Online Audio $19.99

Drumming the Easy Way!

The Beginner's Guide to Playing Drums for Students and Teachers

by Tom Hapke

Cherry Lane Music

Now with online audio! This book takes the beginning drummer through the paces – from reading simple exercises to playing great grooves and fills. Each lesson includes a preparatory exercise and a solo. Concepts and rhythms are introduced one at a time, so growth is natural and easy. Features large, clear musical print, intensive treatment of each individual drum figure, solos following each exercise to motivate students, and more!

02500876 Book/Online Audio $19.99

02500191 Book $12.95

The Drumset Musician – 2nd Edition

by Rod Morgenstein and Rick Mattingly

Containing hundreds of practical, usable beats and fills, *The Drumset Musician* teaches you how to apply a variety of patterns and grooves to the actual performance of songs. The accompanying online audio includes demos as well as 18 play-along tracks covering a wide range of rock, blues and pop styles, with detailed instructions on how to create exciting, solid drum parts.

00268369 Book/Online Audio $19.99

Instant Guide to Drum Grooves

The Essential Reference for the Working Drummer

by Maria Martinez

Become a more versatile drumset player! From traditional Dixieland to cutting-edge hip-hop, *Instant Guide to Drum Grooves* is a handy source featuring 100 patterns that will prepare working drummers for the stylistic variety of modern gigs. The book includes essential beats and grooves in such styles as: jazz, shuffle, country, rock, funk, New Orleans, reggae, calypso, Brazilian and Latin.

06620056 Book/CD Pack $10.99

1001 Drum Grooves

The Complete Resource for Every Drummer

by Steve Mansfield

Cherry Lane Music

This book presents 1,001 drumset beats played in a variety of musical styles, past and present. It's ideal for beginners seeking a well-organized, easy-to-follow encyclopedia of drum grooves, as well as consummate professionals who want to bring their knowledge of various drum styles to new heights. Author Steve Mansfield presents: rock and funk grooves, blues and jazz grooves, ethnic grooves, Afro-Cuban and Caribbean grooves, and much more.

02500337 Book $14.99

Polyrhythms – The Musician's Guide

by Peter Magadini

edited by Wanda Sykes

Peter Magadini's *Polyrhythms* is acclaimed the world over and has been hailed by *Modern Drummer* magazine as "by far the best book on the subject." Written for instrumentalists and vocalists alike, this book with online audio contains excellent solos and exercises that feature polyrhythmic concepts. Topics covered include: 6 over 4, 5 over 4, 7 over 4, 3 over 4, 11 over 4, and other rhythmic ratios; combining various polyrhythms; polyrhythmic time signatures; and much more. The audio includes demos of the exercises and is accessed online using the unique code in each book.

06620053 Book/Online Audio $19.99

Joe Porcaro's Drumset Method – Groovin' with Rudiments

Patterns Applied to Rock, Jazz & Latin Drumset

by Joe Porcaro

Master teacher Joe Porcaro presents rudiments at the drumset in this sensational new edition of *Groovin' with Rudiments*. This book is chock full of exciting drum grooves, sticking patterns, fills, polyrhythmic adaptations, odd meters, and fantastic solo ideas in jazz, rock, and Latin feels. The online audio features 99 audio clip examples in many styles to round out this true collection of superb drumming material for every serious drumset performer.

06620129 Book/Online Audio $24.99

66 Drum Solos for the Modern Drummer

Rock • Funk • Blues • Fusion • Jazz

by Tom Hapke

Cherry Lane Music

66 Drum Solos for the Modern Drummer presents drum solos in all styles of music in an easy-to-read format. These solos are designed to help improve your technique, independence, improvisational skills, and reading ability on the drums and at the same time provide you with some cool licks that you can use right away in your own playing.

02500319 Book/Online Audio $16.99

HAL•LEONARD®

www.halleonard.com

Prices, contents, and availability subject to change without notice.

0120
022